MW01089716

TABLE OF CONTENTS

1	Favorite Scripture about Your Hero
2	Table of Contents
3	Instructions
4	About Me
5-6	About My Scripture Hero
7	Picture
8-9	Quotes
10-13	My Hero at Church
14-17	My Hero's Prayers
18-21	My Hero and Repentance
22-25	My Hero's Appearance
26-29	My Hero at Home
30-33	My Hero and Friends
34-37	My Hero and My Talents
38-41	My Hero and Serving Others
42-45	My Hero and My Language
46-49	My Hero and Sexual Purity
50-53	My Hero and Marriage and Family
54-57	My Hero and Honesty and Integrity
58-61	My Hero and Work and Self-reliance
62-65	My Hero and Health
66-69	My Hero and Entertainment and the Media
70-73	My Hero and Tithing
74-77	My Hero and Education
78-81	My Hero and Scripture Study
82-85	My Hero and Gratitude
86-89	My Hero and Dating
90-93	My Hero and Agency and Accountability
94-96	Wrap Up

INSTRUCTIONS

Step One

Look through the scriptures and make a list of people you admire and look up to.

Some ideas for you are:

Men: Nephi, Lehi, Enos, Samuel the Lamanite, Captain Moroni, Helaman, Abinadi, Ammon, Mormon, Moroni, the brother of Jared, Alma the Younger, Joseph of Egypt, Peter, Paul, Daniel, Moses, John the Baptist, John the Beloved...

Women: Eve, Elisabeth, Sariah, Mary, Mary Magdalene, Rebekah, Sarah, Ruth, Esther, Hannah Naomi, Rachel...

Step Two

Choose a person that you would like to become more like and study in this book. Study their story in the scriptures so you know it well.

Step Three

Get started on this book!

ABOUT ME

My Name: _____

My Age : ....

What is happening in my life right now:

_____

_____

_____

_____

_____

_____

_____

What is happening in the lives of my family members right now:

_____

_____

_____

_____

_____

_____

About My Scripture Hero

The scripture hero I chose is: _____

I can read about them in these books and verses in the scriptures:

WHEN they lived	WHERE they lived

What was happening in the world around him/her (politically, wars, what society was like, etc.):

_____

_____

_____

What I know about their family:

_____

_____

_____

_____

_____

_____

_____

Some significant things that happened in my hero's life are:

_____

_____

_____

_____

_____

_____

Some of my favorite scriptures about my hero are:

Why I chose him/her to be my hero:

_____

_____

_____

_____

_____

Pick your very favorite scripture about your hero and write it out on page one of this book.

MY HERO

Find or draw a picture of your scripture hero and paste it on this page. You can include items or symbols that represent parts of their lives or story.

Find some quotes about your hero and write them on these two pages.

Date: _____

My Hero at Church

"Remember the Sabbath Day to keep it Holy" - Exodus 20:8

What do you think your scripture hero's feelings would be of the Sabbath day?

_____

_____

_____

_____

_____

What do you think your hero's feelings of church would be?

_____

_____

_____

_____

_____

From what you know of your hero's story, what is a specific way that they worshiped Heavenly Father and showed their dedication to Him?

_____

_____

_____

Imagine seeing your hero at church. What do you think they would be doing in the following situations?

Singing the Hymns: _____

During the Sacrament _____

During the Talks _____

In Class _____

In the Hallway _____

Consider what your hero's Sabbath day might look like. Hour by hour, write down what you imagine them doing as they keep the Sabbath day holy (you can look in the *For the Strength of Youth* pamphlet for ideas).

6:00 am	
7:00 am	
8:00 am	
9:00 am	
10:00 am	
11:00 am	
12:00 pm	
1:00 pm	
2:00 pm	
3:00 pm	
4:00 pm	
5:00 pm	
6:00 pm	
7:00 pm	
8:00 pm	
9:00 pm	
10:00 pm	

In what ways would you like to be more like your hero on each Sabbath day?

_____

_____

_____

In this box write your favorite phrase from the *For the Strength of Youth* pamphlet about the Sabbath.

The Sabbath/Church

Find some quotes and scriptures about the Sabbath day or about church that you would like to always remember. Write those quotes in this space. For some good ones to choose from, go to www.theredheadedhostess.com, click on the shopping tab, find this book and click on "Quotes for this Book".

The Sabbath/Church

Write any impressions you had while you were filling out the previous pages. You can include insights you had about the Sabbath and church, thoughts you had about how you can improve, thoughts you had about your hero, goals you would like to make, etc.

Date: _____

My Hero's PRAYERS

"Oh, how praying rests the weary, prayer will change the night to day" – Hymn #140

Take a moment and consider what you think your hero's prayers were like.
Think of six words that you think may have described their prayers.

_____   _____

_____   _____

_____   _____

Take a moment and think of six words that describe YOUR prayers.

_____   _____

_____   _____

_____   _____

From what you know of your hero's story, what are some things they may have prayed about?

_____
_____
_____
_____
_____
_____
_____
_____

What are some things that you often and regularly pray for?

_____
_____
_____
_____
_____
_____
_____

Read the quote to the right and then answer the following questions: After reading that quote, what do you picture your hero's prayers being like?

_____

_____

_____

_____

_____

_____

"As soon as we learn the true relationship in which we stand toward God (namely, God is our Father, and we are his children), then at once prayer becomes natural and instinctive on our part. Many of the so-called difficulties about prayer arise from forgetting this relationship." (Bible Dictionary, 752)

How does understanding your relationship with Heavenly Father influence your prayers? How could thinking about this improve your prayers?

_____

_____

_____

_____

Look up the following scriptures. Choose one that you would like to describe your prayers and color it in.

Matthew 6:7   James 1:6

Enos 1:4

Alma 37:37   Alma 5:46

Doctrine & Covenants 10:5

PRAYER

Find some quotes and scriptures about PRAYER that you would like to always remember. Write those quotes in this space. For some options to choose from, go to www.theredheadedhostess.com, click on the shopping tab, find this book and click on "Quotes for this Book".

PRAYER

Write any impressions you had while you were filling out the previous pages. You can include insights you had about PRAYER, thoughts you had about how you can improve, thoughts you had about your hero, goals you would like to make, etc.

My Hero and Repentance

Look up the scriptures below. In the box beside the scripture write what your hero would want you to understand about repentance in that scripture.

Isaiah 1:18	
Alma 34:33-34	
Isaiah 53:3-5	
Doctrine and Covenants 19:16-19	

In this box write your favorite phrase from the *For the Strength of Youth* pamphlet about "Repentance".

How often do you think your hero repented?

_____

_____

_____

What sort of things do you think your hero may have repented of?

_____

_____

_____

In what ways do you think repentance played a role in their becoming so great?

_____

_____

What if your hero had not chosen to humble themselves and repent of their shortcomings? How would that have impacted their life?

_____

_____

_____

From everything that you have studied and considered about repentance, how could you better use the power of repentance in your life?

_____

_____

_____

_____

How can repentance help you become truly great, like your hero?

_____

_____

_____

_____

Repentance

Find some quotes and scriptures about REPENTANCE that you would like to remember. Write those quotes in this space. For good ones to choose from, go to www.theredheadedhostess.com, click on the shopping tab, find this book and click on "Quotes for this Book".

Repentance

Write any impressions you had while you were filling out the previous pages. You can include insights you had about REPENTANCE, thoughts you had about how you can improve, thoughts you had about your hero, goals you would like to make, etc.

Date: _____

My Hero and their APPEARANCE

What do you imagine your hero looked like?

_____

_____

_____

What do you think were some of the styles in the day they lived?

_____

_____

_____

What do you think may have been some of the challenges, pressures, or worldly temptations they faced when it came to styles, clothing or appearance?

_____

_____

_____

If your hero were living in the world TODAY, how do you imagine they would look (dress, hair, etc.)?

_____

_____

_____

What are some of the challenges they would confront in today's world concerning style and appearance?

_____

_____

_____

_____

Look up "Dress and Appearance" in the *For the Strength of Youth* pamphlet. Find 7 principles that stand out to you and write them in the left column. Then in the right column write how you imagine your hero would be an example of that statement.

Statement	How you imagine your hero being an example of this

Why is it important that you, like your hero, live the principles above?

_____

_____

_____

_____

APPEARANCE

Find some quotes and scriptures about APPEARANCE, MODESTY, ETC. that you would like to always remember. Write those quotes in this space. For some good ones to choose from, go to www.theredheadedhostess.com, click on the shopping tab, find this book and click on "Quotes for this Book".

APPEARANCE

Write any impressions you had while you were filling out the previous pages. You can include insights you had about this topic, thoughts you had about how you can improve, thoughts you had about your hero, goals you would like to make, etc.

Date: _____

My Hero at  HOME

From what you know of your hero's story, in what ways were they loving and serving their current (or future) family?

_____
_____
_____

Imagine visiting your hero's home. Consider the following things:

What do you imagine their home being like?

_____
_____
_____
_____
_____

How do you think you would feel in their home?

_____
_____
_____
_____
_____

If they lived today, what are some things they would definitely have in their home?

_____
_____
_____
_____

If they lived today, what are some things they would definitely not have in their home?

_____
_____
_____
_____

Now imagine your own home (or even just your personal bedroom), consider the following things:

How do people feel when they are there?

_____
_____
_____
_____
_____

What are specific things I have that communicate that this is a place of peace and refuge from the world?

_____
_____
_____
_____

What are things I may have or do that distract from the Spirit and love in our home?

_____
_____
_____
_____

What are specific things can I do to make our home more of a place of peace and refuge?

_____
_____
_____
_____

How does the feeling in my home make a difference on how we act outside of the home?

_____
_____
_____
_____

How would my hero feel in my home and what advice might they give?

_____
_____
_____
_____

If you were to hang a scripture over your front door that represents what you want your family to represent, which one would you choose? Color it in.

Joshua 24:15   Romans 1:16   1 Nephi 3:7

Doctrine and Covenants 93:40

Helaman 5:12   Moroni 7:45, 47

Find some quotes and scriptures about HOME that you would like to remember. Write those quotes in this space. For some good ones to choose from, go to www.theredheadedhostess.com, click on the shopping tab, find this book and click on "Quotes for this Book".

Write any impressions you had while you were filling out the previous pages. You can include insights you had about HOME, thoughts you had about how you can improve, thoughts you had about your hero, goals you would like to make, etc.

Date: _____

My Hero and Friends

From what you know of your hero's story, who were the people they were friends with?

_____

_____

What are some things they did to lift and be a good friend to those that you wrote above?

_____

_____

Who are some other friends they may have had in their life that aren't mentioned in the scriptures?

_____

_____

Look up "Friends" in the *For the Strength of Youth* pamphlet. Fill in the blank in the left column. In the right column, write why your hero would have lived that principle.

STATEMENT	WHY YOUR HERO WOULD HAVE LIVED THIS PRINCIPLE
Choose your friends _____	
Choose friends who share your _____	
A true friend will encourage you to be _____	
To have good friends, be a good _____ _____	

How do you think your hero's friends contributed to his or her greatness?

_____

_____

In what ways do you think your hero contributed to their friends' greatness?

_____

_____

Think of some of your closest friends. Pick three of them and write them in the boxes on the left side below. Then in the center box write what you hope their life will be like ten years from now. Finally, in the right box, think about and then write what you could do now (as a true friend) to help them achieve their greatness.

FRIEND	THEIR LIFE IN 10 YEARS	WHAT YOU CAN DO

Turn to "Friends" in your *For the Strength of Youth* pamphlet and write your favorite phrase in this space.

Friends

Find some quotes and scriptures about FRIENDS that you would like to remember. Write those quotes in this space. For good ones to choose from, go to www.theredheadedhostess.com, click on the shopping tab, find this book and click on "Quotes for this Book".

Friends

Write any impressions you had while you were filling out the previous pages. You can include insights you had about FRIENDS, thoughts you had about how you can improve, thoughts you had about your hero, goals you would like to make, etc.

Date: _____

My Hero and MY TALENTS

What sacred and glorious purpose was your hero sent to earth to do?

_____
_____
_____
_____

What are some of the talents and abilities that Heavenly Father blessed your hero with so that they could fulfill their mission?

_____
_____
_____
_____

What do you hope your sacred and glorious purpose on earth is?

_____
_____
_____

Sometimes it is hard for us to recognize our gifts and abilities because they come so natural to us. Fill out the following below to see if you can identify some of your special gifts that you have been blessed with.

What are some things you are naturally drawn to learning about? For example, if you are looking through a magazine, what kind of articles would you stop to read?

_____
_____
_____

What are talents, abilities, and traits that people compliment you on?

_____
_____
_____

What are things that come easy to you that may not always be easy for others?

_____
_____
_____
_____

What are abilities that your family points out to you? (go and ask them if you need to)

_____
_____
_____
_____

In the chart below is a list of roles that you will likely have some, most or all of your life. In the middle box list the strengths and gifts that you listed on the last page that will help you act well in that role and make a positive difference. In the box next to it think of things that you could still pray for and develop and write those in that box.

Roles you will play	Skills, strengths, and talents I have	Skills, strengths, and talents I need
Daughter		
Sister		
Friend		
Student		
Missionary/Example		
Employee		
Wife		
Mother		
Teacher in the home		
Teacher/Leader in church		
Neighbor		

Becoming a powerful person like your hero takes a lot of work. Considering what you wrote on the last page about what you hope your purpose on earth is, **what are some strengths and talents that you would like to work on in order to make a difference like your hero?**

MY TALENTS

Find some quotes and scriptures about TALENTS that you would like to remember. Write those quotes in this space. For good ones to choose from, go to www.theredheadedhostess.com, click on the shopping tab, find this book and click on "Quotes for this Book".

MY TALENTS

Write any impressions you had while you were filling out the previous pages. You can include insights you had about TALENTS, thoughts you had about how you can improve, thoughts you had about your hero, goals you would like to make, etc.

Date: _____

My Hero and Serving others

From what you know of your hero's story, what are some ways he or she was of service to others?

_____

_____

_____

In what ways did their serving others also serve Heavenly Father?

_____

_____

_____

How do you think having a life filled with service impacted who your hero became?

_____

_____

_____

Below are some circumstances your hero may have found themselves in. Consider how they would have served others in each scenario and write down your thoughts in the right column.

Scenarios	How your hero would have served
In the hallways at school	
With their siblings at home	
With their parents at home	
With their classes at church	
In their neighborhood	
To the less fortunate	

Consider the following scenarios below. Think of ways that you could be of great service in each situation and then write your thoughts in the middle column. Finally, in the right column write how that would also be serving Heavenly Father (Mosiah 2:17).

Scenarios	How I could be of great service	How this is also serving Heavenly Father
With your family in the morning		
With a specific neighbor		
To one of your leaders or teachers at church		
Before a church activity		
After a church activity		
With your extended family		

How would serving more often and more thoughtfully impact the kind of person you become and help you fulfill your life's mission?

_____

_____

_____

Turn to "Service" in your *For the Strength of Youth* pamphlet and write your favorite phrase in this space.

serving others

Find some quotes and scriptures about SERVING OTHERS that you would like to remember. Write those quotes in this space. For some good ones go to www.theredheadedhostess.com, click on the shopping tab, find this book and click on "Quotes for this Book".

Write any impressions you had while you were filling out the previous pages. You can include insights you had about SERVING OTHERS, thoughts you had about how you can improve, thoughts you had about your hero, goals you would like to make, etc.

Date: _____

My Hero and My Language

Turn to your hero's story in the scriptures. Find some times when they spoke and then pick 6 words that they used that contain a lot of power.

1 _____   4 _____

2 _____   5 _____

3 _____   6 _____

Below are phrases from the *For the Strength of Youth* pamphlet under "Language". See if you can fill in the blanks with the correct words and then check them by looking it up in your own pamphlet. Then answer the provided questions about your hero.

How you communicate should reflect who you are as a _____.

How do those 6 words above reflect that your hero knows that he or she is a child of God?

How do you picture your hero communicating with others? Think of specific things they would or would not have done.

Help others improve their language by your _____.

Besides your scripture hero, who is someone in your life that is a good example of having excellent language? What do they do? How does their example impact others?

Choose not to insult others or put them down, even in _____.

What are some common ways that we jokingly insult others and put them down?

Why would your hero **not** do this?

Avoid _____ of any kind, and avoid speaking in _____.

Why would your hero not gossip about others?

If your hero were talking about someone when they were not present, what kind of things would you imagine your hero saying?

Why would your hero avoid speaking in anger?

Always use the name of God and Jesus Christ with _____.

In what kind of situations would your hero use the names of God and Jesus Christ?

Remember that these standards for your use of language apply to all forms of communication, including _____.

If your hero lived in today's world how would he use all of these other forms of communication?

What would your hero avoid doing when it comes to the language they use in these other forms of communication?

Words hold a lot of power and they can do a lot of good but they can also do a lot of bad. Below are some scriptures, look them up and under each scripture consider and then write what those scriptures teach your about LANGUAGE.

James 3:2-10	Matthew 15:11	Ephesians 4:29-32	Enos 1:3

My Language

Find some quotes and scriptures about LANGUAGE that you would like to remember. Write those quotes in this space. For some good ones go to www.theredheadedhostess.com, click on the shopping tab, find this book and click on "Quotes for this Book".

My Language

Write any impressions you had while you were filling out the previous pages. You can include insights you had about LANGUAGE, thoughts you had about how you can improve, thoughts you had about your hero, goals you would like to make, etc.

Date: _____

My Hero and SEXUAL PURITY

Below are phrases from the *For the Strength of Youth* pamphlet about "Sexual Purity". Consider each statement and then write how your hero's life would have been an example of that statement.

Statement	How your hero's life would have been an example of this principle or doctrine
Physical intimacy between husband and wife is beautiful and sacred	
God has commanded that sexual intimacy be reserved for marriage	
When you are sexually pure... you prepare yourself to build a strong marriage	
When you are sexually pure... you protect yourself from spiritual and emotional damage	
Remaining sexually pure... improves your ability to make good decisions now and in the future	
The Lord's standard regarding sexual purity is clear and unchanging	
Never do anything that could lead to sexual transgression	
Avoid situations that invite increased temptation	
Have faith in and be obedient to the righteous counsel of your parents and leaders	

Consider the following situations. Write how you imagine your hero behaving in each of them.

They realize that the movie they are at has sexual content

As a teenager their friends are going on an overnighter without adult supervision

Their friend tells an inappropriate joke

While on the internet an inappropriate site comes up

They want to make personal and specific standards on the messages in their music

After they are married they make specific goals to be completely faithful to their spouse

If you were asked to give a talk about the importance of "sexual purity" what is a scripture you would use? Write that scripture in this space.

SEXUAL PURITY

Find some quotes and scriptures about SEXUAL PURITY that you would like to remember. Write those quotes in this space. For some good ones go to www.theredheadedhostess.com, click on the shopping tab, find this book and click on "Quotes for this Book".

sexual purity

Write any impressions you had while you were filling out the previous pages. You can include insights you had about SEXUAL PURTY, thoughts you had about how you can improve, thoughts you had about your hero, goals you would like to make, etc.

Date: _____

My Hero and Marriage & Family

What are specifics you know about your hero and their family?

_____
_____
_____
_____

What would you expect your hero's view on family would be?

_____
_____
_____
_____
_____
_____

What would you expect your hero's view on marriage would be?

_____
_____
_____
_____
_____

As a teenager, what things do you imagine your hero doing to prepare themselves for their future marriage and family?

_____
_____
_____
_____
_____

After your hero was married, what kinds of things do you think he or she did to ensure that their marriage was strong and their family happy?

_____
_____
_____
_____
_____

Look up the standard "Family" in your *For the Strength of Youth* pamphlet. There are five wonderful paragraphs that talk about this standard.
- In each paragraph pick out one statement that really stands out to you and write it in the left column.
- In the right column write how you imagine your hero being an example of what you wrote.

Statement	How you imagine your hero being an example of this
①	
②	
③	
④	
⑤	

Pick one statement above and consider how your life could be a great example of that statement.

Marriage & Family

Find some quotes and scriptures about MARRIAGE & FAMILY that you would like to remember. Write those quotes in this space. For some good ones go to www.theredheadedhostess.com, click on the shopping tab, find this book and click on "Quotes for this Book".

Marriage & Family

Write any impressions you had while you were filling out the previous pages. You can include insights you had about MARRIAGE AND FAMILY, thoughts you had about how you can improve, thoughts you had about your hero, goals you would like to make, etc.

My Hero and Honesty & Integrity

Look up in a dictionary the words below. Write their definitions beside the words.

Honesty: _____

Integrity: _____

From what you know of your hero's story, when were some times when he or she were examples of what you wrote above?

_____
_____
_____
_____

Why do you think being honest and having integrity contributed to your hero becoming such a great person?

_____
_____
_____
_____

How could dishonesty or not having integrity have impacted your hero's story?

_____
_____
_____
_____

Pick four phrases in the *For the Strength of Youth* pamphlet under "Honesty and Integrity" that you think your hero would have been an example of and write them below.

①

②

③

④

When are some instances in your life that you were also an example of those statements?

How would being an **excellent example** of those statements have an impact on your life?

Honesty and Integrity

Find some quotes and scriptures about HONESTY & INTEGRITY that you would like to always remember and write them in this space. For some good ones go to www.theredheadedhostess.com, click on the shopping tab, find this book and click on "Quotes for this Book".

Honesty and Integrity

My Hero and Work

Knowing what you do about your hero's life, what type of things would they have needed to work hard for?

_____

_____

_____

_____

In what ways do you think being a hard worker impacted your hero's life and who he or she became? What if they had not developed this quality?

_____

_____

_____

_____

Turn to "Work and Self-Reliance" in your For the Strength of Youth pamphlet. Pick 6 phrases that you think your hero lived by.

1-   4-

2-   5-

3-   6-

Turn to Matthew 25:14-29. In the spaces below draw what is happening in the verses at the base of each box. Use a dictionary to look up words you do not understand.

Matthew 25:14-15	25:16	25:17	25:18	25:19

25:20-21	25:22-23	25:24-27	25:28	25:29

In what ways do you feel your hero was like the servant with five talents?

_____

_____

_____

_____

Read the second to last paragraph in your *For the Strength of Youth* pamphlet about "self-reliance". How was your hero an example of this paragraph?

_____

_____

_____

_____

Work & Self-Reliance

Find some quotes and scriptures about WORK & SELF-RELIANCE that you would like to always remember and write them in this space. For some good ones go to www.theredheadedhostess.com, click on the shopping tab, find this book and click on "Quotes for this Book".

Work & Self-Reliance

Write any impressions you had while you were filling out the previous pages. You can include insights you had about WORK AND SELF-RELIANCE, thoughts you had about how you can improve, thoughts you had about your hero, goals you would like to make, etc.

My Hero and HEALTH

With everything your hero needed to accomplish, why would good health play an important role in their success?

_____

_____

_____

_____

_____

Make a list of phrases from the For the Strength of Youth pamphlet under "Health" that you think your hero would have lived by.

What are some things that you do to have good physical and emotional health, that you feel your hero also would have done?

_____

_____

_____

_____

What are some additional things that your hero might advise you that you could do?

_____

_____

_____

_____

How does having good physical and emotional health impact how you feel spiritually and how much you can accomplish?

_____

_____

_____

_____

How does having good physical and emotional health impact your relationships with those you care the most about and how you feel about yourself?

_____

_____

_____

_____

_____

HEALTH

Find some quotes and scriptures about HEALTH that you would like to remember. Write those quotes in this space. For some good ones to choose from, go to www.theredheadedhostess.com, click on the shopping tab, find this book and click on "Quotes for this Book".

HEALTH

Write any impressions you had while you were filling out the previous pages. You can include insights you had about HEALTH., thoughts you had about how you can improve, thoughts you had about your hero, goals you would like to make, etc.

My Hero and Entertainment & Media

What kind of entertainment do you think existed in your hero's day?

_____

_____

What are some ways you think Satan may have tried to corrupt the entertainment back then?

_____

_____

What are some things you think your hero may have done to safeguard themselves against harmful entertainment?

_____

_____

> Fill in the blank in the following statements from the *For the Strength of Youth* pamphlet under "Entertainment and Media".

The information and entertainment provided through these media can increase your ability to _____, communicate, and become a force for _____ in the world.

Choose wisely when using media, because whatever you_____, _____, or _____ at has an _____ you.

Satan uses media to deceive you by making what is wrong and evil look _____, _____, or _____.

_____ in all forms is especially dangerous and _____.

Avoid _____ at all costs. It is a _____ that weakens your _____, destroys your feelings of _____ and changes the way you see _____.

Take care that your use of media does not dull your _____ to the Spirit or interfere with your personal _____ with others.

Spending long periods of time using the _____ or a _____ device, playing _____ _____, or watching _____ or other media can keep you from valuable interactions with other _____.

Be careful that your use of _____ _____ does not replace spending time with your _____ and _____.

Do not communicate anything over the _____ or through _____ that would be inappropriate to share in _____.

Obey the _____ that govern sharing _____, movies, and other items.

If there is anything VIRTUOUS, lovely, or of

good report or praiseworthy,

we seek after these things.

Article of Faith #13

Below are some forms of media and entertainment. Come up with THREE specific examples under each item that your hero would read, listen to, watch or play.

Television Programs:

Movies:

Music Groups:

Internet Sites:

Books:

Video Games:

Entertainment & Media

Find some quotes and scriptures about ENTERTAINMENT & MEDIA that you would like to remember and write them in this space. For some good ones go to www.theredheadedhostess.com, click on the shopping tab, find this book and click on "Quotes for this Book".

Entertainment & Media

Write any impressions you had while you were filling out the previous pages. You can include insights you had about ENTERTAINMENT AND MEDIA., thoughts you had about how you can improve, thoughts you had about your hero, goals you would like to make, etc.

Date: _____

My Hero and *Tithing*

What kind of an attitude toward tithing do you think your hero had?

_____

_____

_____

When do you think your hero would set his tithing aside? Before or after he took care of other financial needs and wants? Why?

_____

_____

_____

How often do you think your hero paid their tithing? Why?

_____

_____

_____

If your hero lived today, what kind of things would their tithing be used for? (Use the *For the Strength of Youth pamphlet* for some ideas).

_____

_____

_____

Why would those things you wrote above be important to your hero? And why would they be more important than some other things your hero may want to spend their money on?

_____

_____

_____

_____

What kind of blessings do you think your hero experienced because he or she paid their tithing?

_____
_____
_____
_____

If you were asked to put a scripture inside your tithing envelope that explains how you feel about tithing, which one would you choose? Color in the scripture you would choose.

Malachi 3:10   Proverbs 3:9   Jacob 2:17-19

Pick a phrase that really stands out to you about "Tithing" in the *For the Strength of Youth* pamphlet and write it in this space.

Tithing

Find some quotes and scriptures about TITHING that you would like to remember. Write those quotes in this space. For some good ones go to www.theredheadedhostess.com, click on the shopping tab, find this book and click on "Quotes for this Book".

Tithing

Write any impressions you had while you were filling out the previous pages. You can include insights you had about TITHING., thoughts you had about how you can improve, thoughts you had about your hero, goals you would like to make, etc.

Date: _____

My Hero and EDUCATION

Read "Education" in your *For the Strength of Youth* pamphlet and then answer the questions below applying the principles you just read along with your own thoughts and insights.

Why would education be an <u>eternally</u> important thing to your hero?

_____
_____
_____

What would your hero do to "educate [their] mind"?

_____
_____
_____

What would your hero do to "develop [their] skills and talents"?

_____
_____
_____

Why would your hero want to develop the "power to act well in [their] responsibilities" (home, work, callings, school, family, etc.)?

_____
_____
_____

How would an education impact your hero's life?

_____
_____
_____

If your hero lived in today's world, what do you think he or she would act like at school? How would they approach learning their various subjects? How would they treat the teachers?

What kind of advice would your hero give someone who was still in school?

In what ways do you imagine your hero continuing to learn and increase in knowledge and skill **after** their formal education was complete?

In what ways do you think your hero focused on their spiritual education?

What specific advice do you think your hero might give you about this standard?

EDUCATION

Find some quotes and scriptures about EDUCATION that you would like to always remember. Write those quotes in this space. For some good ones go to www.theredheadedhostess.com, click on the shopping tab, find this book and click on "Quotes for this Book".

EDUCATION

My Hero and Scripture Study

From what you know of your hero's story and of the time that he or she lived, how do you think your hero learned the Gospel?

_____

_____

_____

If your hero lived in today's world, what would he or she marvel at when it comes to specific things available in learning and studying the Gospel?

_____

_____

_____

If your hero lived today and had all of the available resources, what would you picture their scripture study being like?

_____

_____

_____

_____

How do you think your hero's study of the Gospel impacted their life and their relationships?

_____

_____

_____

_____

How would studying your scriptures like the way you imagine your hero studying their scriptures impact your life, your family and your future family?

_____

_____

_____

_____

_____

_____

Consider the following questions and then write how you feel it could help you improve your scripture study.

What time of day are you most alert and able to learn?	
What resources are available that can help you understand the scriptures better?	
Where is a place in your home that you can best concentrate?	
What are some things that you can do to help you better concentrate and learn?	
What are some things you could do to remember what you are learning?	

Write some GOALS you feel would make your scripture study more meaningful

Scripture Study

Find some quotes and scriptures about SCRIPTURE STUDY that you would like to always remember and write them in this space. For some good ones go to www.theredheadedhostess.com, click on the shopping tab, find this book and click on "Quotes for this Book".

Scripture Study

Write any impressions you had while you were filling out the previous pages. You can include insights you had about SCRIPTURE STUDY., thoughts you had about how you can improve, thoughts you had about your hero, goals you would like to make, etc.

Date: _____

My Hero and GRATITUDE

From what you know of your hero's story what are some things he or she likely would have been grateful for?

_____
_____
_____

From what you know of your hero's story, what were some of their difficult times?

_____
_____
_____

Even during your hero's difficult times, what did they have to be grateful for?

_____
_____
_____

How did your hero's life show Heavenly Father that they were grateful to Him for all that he or she had??

_____
_____
_____

How did being a grateful person impact the kind of person your hero became?

_____
_____
_____

Pick a phrase that really stands out to you about "GRATITUDE" in the *For the Strength of Youth* pamphlet and write it in this space.

Consider the following questions and then write your answers in the right column.

What are some things you are really grateful for?	
During some difficult times, what did you have to be grateful for?	
What are some strengths you have that you are grateful for?	
How does your life reflect to Heavenly Father that you are grateful for what you have?	
How does being grateful impact the kind of person you are becoming?	

GRATITUDE

Find some quotes and scriptures about GRATITUDE that you would like to remember. Write those quotes in this space. For some good ones go to www.theredheadedhostess.com, click on the shopping tab, find this book and click on "Quotes for this Book".

GRATITUDE

Write any impressions you had while you were filling out the previous pages. You can include insights you had about GRATITUDE., thoughts you had about how you can improve, thoughts you had about your hero, goals you would like to make, etc.

Date: _____

My Hero and DATING

As your hero approached dating years, what do you think his or her view of an appropriate boy/girl relationship would look like?

_____
_____
_____
_____

What are some *Gospel doctrines* that would influence the kind of choices your hero would make in their dating decisions?

_____
_____
_____
_____

How would proper dating help them reach his or her goal of having an Eternal marriage?

_____
_____
_____
_____

Look up "Dating" in your *For the Strength of Youth* pamphlet and answer the following:

What is a date?

What can dating help the youth do?

Consider the following questions discussed in your *For the Strength of Youth* pamphlet and then write what you think your hero would do in the right column.

Why would your hero wait until they were 16 to date?	
What are some personal rules they would have for dating?	
What kind of people would they go on dates with?	
What would an average date look like?	
How would your hero ask, accept or decline a date?	
What would their dating look like in their young adult years?	
How would they be a righteous influence on those they go on dates with?	
In what ways would appropriate dating influence their relationship with their future spouse?	

DATING

Find some quotes and scriptures about DATING that you would like to always remember. Write those quotes in this space. For some good ones go to www.theredheadedhostess.com, click on the shopping tab, find this book and click on "Quotes for this Book".

DATiNG

Write any impressions you had while you were filling out the previous pages. You can include insights you had about DATING., thoughts you had about how you can improve, thoughts you had about your hero, goals you would like to make, etc.

Date: _____

My Hero and Agency & Accountability

From what you know of your hero's story, what are some **specific righteous choices** that he or she made?

_____

_____

Look up the definition of "consequence" and write it in this space.
CONSEQUENCE:

What are some of your hero's consequences to those choices?

_____

_____

_____

_____

Being **accountable** means that you are willing to answer for the choices you have made, good or bad. When we are bad we don't lie or blame others. **Why would this be an important characteristic for your hero to have?**

_____

_____

_____

Pick a phrase that really stands out to you about "AGENCY AND ACCOUNTABILITY" in the *For the Strength of Youth* pamphlet and write it in this space.

Now that you have studied your hero in such depth, look through your book and choose some of the choices he or she made (real choices or ones you imagined they would make) that you would also like to make in your life and then write what consequences you would hope to get from those choices.

Choice	What consequences I would like to have in my life from this choice

Agency & Accountability

Find some quotes and scriptures about AGENCY & ACCOUNTABILITY that you would like to remember and write them in this space. For some good ones go to www.theredheadedhostess.com, click on the shopping tab, find this book and click on "Quotes for this Book".

Agency & Accountability

Write any impressions you had while you were filling out the previous pages. You can include insights you had about AGENCY AND ACCOUNTABILITY., thoughts you had about how you can improve, thoughts you had about your hero, goals you would like to make, etc.

Congratulations on finishing the book! To wrap up everything you have learned, finish the following sentences below.

If I had to explain what kind of a person my scripture hero was I would say...

_____

_____

_____

_____

_____

_____

_____

Some of my favorite pages I studied in this book are...

_____

_____

_____

_____

_____

_____

_____

_____

_____

Some things I learned about the standards in the *For the Strength of Youth* are...

_____
_____
_____
_____
_____
_____
_____
_____
_____
_____
_____

Some changes I have made by following my hero's example are...

_____
_____
_____
_____
_____
_____
_____
_____
_____
_____
_____
_____

I think Heavenly Father wanted this person in the scriptures because...

_____

_____

_____

_____

_____

_____

_____

_____

_____

_____

_____

_____

I want to become more like my scripture hero. To make this happen I will...

_____

_____

_____

_____

_____

_____

_____

_____

_____

_____

_____

_____

Made in the USA
Charleston, SC
06 February 2015